Jimi's Book of Japanese
A Motivating Method to Learn Japanese™ (Katakana)

FIRST PB&J OMNIMEDIA™ EDITION 2005

Published in the United States by PB&J Omnimedia™
A division of Takahashi & Black™

Jimi's Book of Japanese: A Motivating Method to Learn Japanese™ *(Katakana)*

Design and layout copyright ©2005 by Yumie Toka
Illustrations copyright ©2005 by Yumie Toka
Text copyright ©2005 by Peter X. Takahashi

All rights reserved. No part of this book may be reproduced, stored in a retrieval system, or transmitted in any form or by any means, electronic, photocopying, recording or otherwise, without prior written permission from the publisher.

PB&J Omnimedia™ Triple Bubble Learning System™, Supaa Rare™, characters, names, logos and indicia are trademarks and/or registered trademarks of PB&J Omnimedia™ and Takahashi & Black™. For licensing information, please contact us.

Library of Congress Cataloging-in-Publication Data available.

ISBN 0-9723247-2-0

Printed in Singapore

Typeset in Adobe Frutiger and Hiragino

A PB&J Omnimedia™ book

10 9 8 7 6 5 4 3 2 1

PB&J Omnimedia™ products are available at special discounts for bulk purchases in the United States by corporations, institutions and people named Mojo. For international discount programs and other information, please contact us.

PB&J Omnimedia™
www.pbjomnimedia.com

Jimi's Book of Japanese
A Motivating Method to Learn Japanese™ (Katakana)

Peter X. Takahashi
Illustrations by Yumie Toka
Edited by Mikki Moto

About *kana*

Instead of an alphabet, Japanese uses *kana*. Each *kana* represents a syllable. There are two kinds of *kana*: *hiragana* and *katakana*. *Hiragana* is used for the traditional sounds of Japanese. *Katakana* is used for words Japanese has borrowed from other languages. Both *kana* sets are what you use when you first learn Japanese.

These two sets are mixed with Chinese characters, called *kanji*. Each *kanji* represents a word or idea and may be pronounced several different ways depending on its use. There are thousands of *kanji*. It takes many years to learn them so it is best to master *kana* while learning a few *kanji* at a time.

There are many ways to transliterate *kana*. All *kana* in this book are matched with *romaji*, a script used to teach Japanese to foreigners. Below is a guide to help you pronounce *romaji*.

About pronunciation
Vowels

Japanese has five vowel sounds and it takes a bit of practice to learn them. On every page, you'll find a pronunciation key. Wherever you see the key, say:

"a" as in f**a**ther "i" as in **i**nk "u" as in fl**u**te "e" as in **e**nd "o" as in **o**atmeal

A bar over a vowel means that the sound is long. Say *obāsan* (grandma), not *obasan* (aunt).

When you see vowel pairs: say **ie** as "ee-eh"; say **ee** as "eh-eh"; say **oo** as "o-oo"; say **ae** as "ah-eh"; say **ei** like the "ay" in "day"; say **ai** like "Thai".

Other things you need to know

For other sounds, say them as you normally would, but with these tips in mind:
   g sounds like "g" in "go";
   r sounds more like "l";
   fu sounds halfway between "foo" and "hoo";
   n sound is a nasal "n" sound, said as if you had a stuffy nose;
   (w)o sound is shown with "w" in brackets because you write "wo", but say "o".

Stress

In Japanese, you say each part of a word with equal stress. Say e-da-ma-me, not e-da-MA-me.

Writing Japanese

Proper stroke order is from left to right and top to bottom. Normally, horizontal strokes are written before vertical strokes.

SAVE JIMI!

With Jimi feeling under the weather, Dizzy Fugu, the magical puffer fish, needs your help. Meet Dizzy in the operating room . . . STAT! Use your skill and brainpower to cure Jimi's ailments while having a blast learning vital vocabulary words.

You can almost taste how fun this is going to be, can't you?

ディジーフグ ↗
dizzy fugu

About this book

This is the second book in the award winning *Jimi's Book of Japanese* series designed for everyone who is learning Japanese and for anyone who has an inquisitive brain.

The Japanese *kana* taught in this book are *katakana*, the sounds Japanese has borrowed from other languages. Don't worry. They're easy to learn. With this book's special **Triple Bubble Learning System**™, you'll learn *kana* quickly and easily. Just follow the simple steps below.

First, look at the pronunciation key and say the *kana* sound aloud. Then, look at the giant *kana* and say its sound three times as you trace it with your finger—this helps *kana* stick in your brain. Next, read the word next to the *kana*. Then, look for its picture or definition. Matching *kana* with words, pictures and definitions makes *kana* unforgettable, and it's fun.

Each page is specially designed with six user-friendly features:

1. **Giant *kana*** helps you fix its shape in your brain. Inside, stroke order arrows help you develop accurate style.

2. **Pronunciation key** teaches you to say each sound in a really Japanese way.

3. **Japanese-English vocabulary** are linked with colorful illustrations; simple definitions make them easy to remember.

4. **Page numbers** in Japanese teach you how to count from 1 to 52.

5. **Authentic descriptions** about Japanese culture and customs help you remember *kana* and increase your knowledge of Japan.

6. **Color-coding** for each *kana* set allows you to study *kana* together or separately.

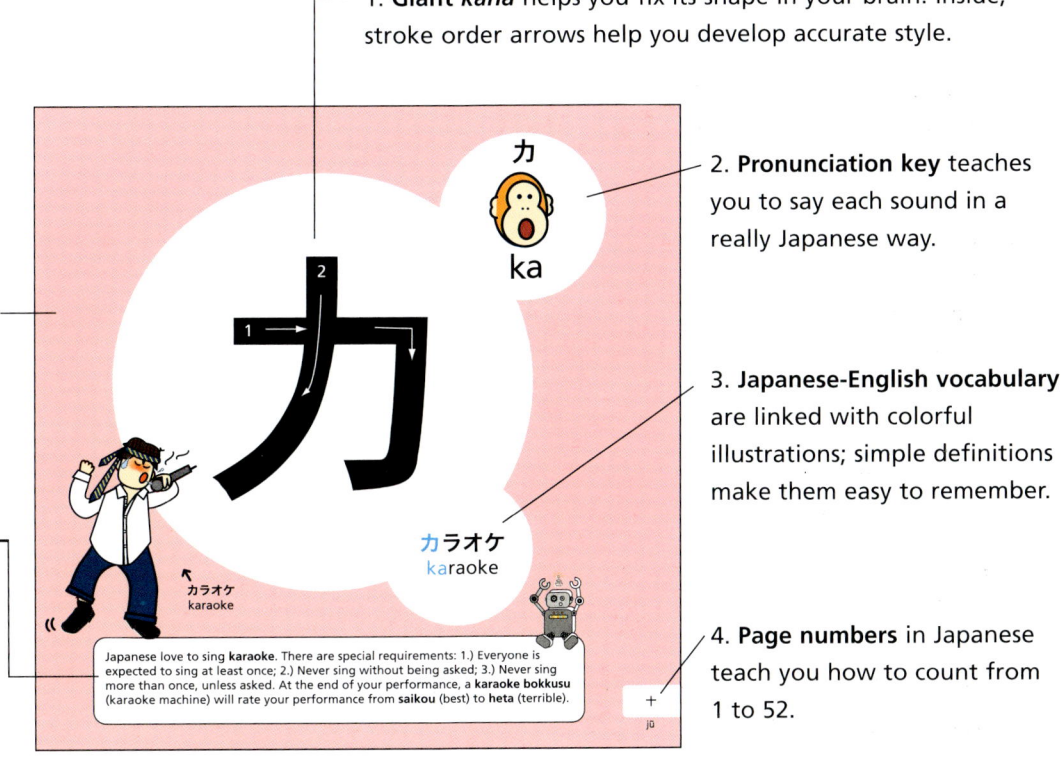

In the back, there's a word list with definitions, colorful numbers page, lively visual library and color-coded *katakana* table. Use this material to quickly review what you've learned in this book.

ア
a

アニメ キャラクター
anime kyarakutā

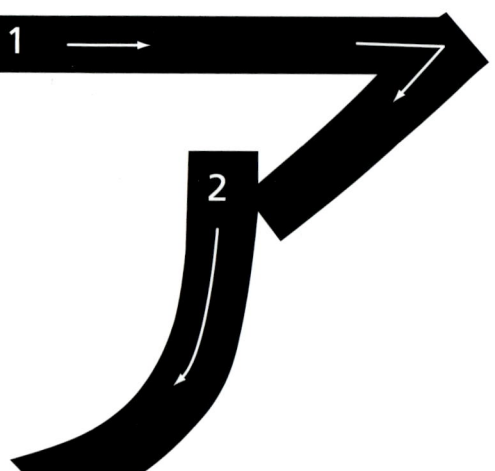

アニメ
anime

アニメ キャラクター
anime kyarakutā

Pokemon®, Dragon Ball Z® and G-Force® are all examples of **anime**, a tremendously popular form of stylish Japanimation. Anime **kyarakutā** (characters) are easily recognizable by their tiny noses, sparkly eyes and larger-than-life expressions. Japan's highest-grossing film is *Spirited Away*, a traditional anime by Hayao Miyazaki.

Pokemon® Nintendo of America; Dragon Ball Z® Toei Animation Co., LTD; G-Force® Tatsunoko Production Co.

イ 
i

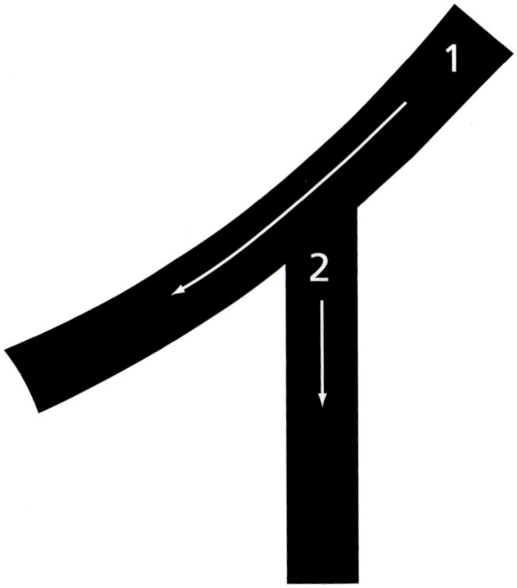

インターネット
intānetto

メディア メール
media mēru

More than 40 million Japanese subscribe to i-mode®, an innovative keitai denwa service by NTT DoCoMo. With i-mode®, users get easy access to 66,000 **intānetto** (Internet) sites, services such as **media mēru** (media mail), restaurant advice and online banking. Users can access i-mode® from anywhere in Japan, usually at low cost.

i-mode® NTT DoCoMo

六
roku

ウ
u

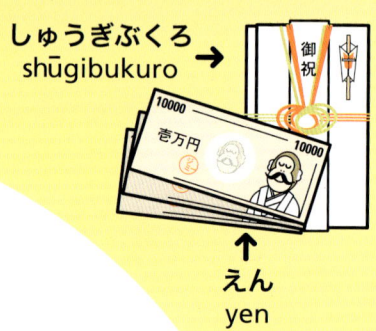

しゅうぎぶくろ
shūgibukuro

えん
yen

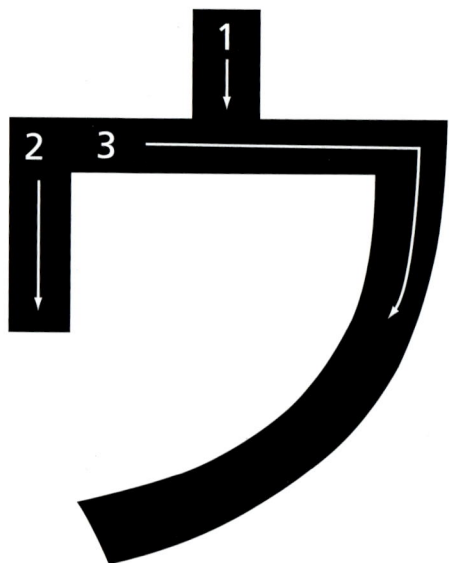

ウエディング
uedingu

もんつき
montsuki

つのかくし
tsunokakushi

ぶんきんたかしまだ
bunkintakashimada

しろむく
shiromuku

There are Shinto, Buddhist and Christian **uedingu** (weddings) in Japan. At a traditional ceremony, the groom wears a formal **montsuki** (black kimono with family crest), while the bride wears a **shiromuku** (white kimono) and elegant **bunkintakashimada** (special hairdo). At the reception, guests give **shūgibukuro**, a decorative envelope stuffed with **yen**.

エ
e

エレベーター
erebētā

エレベーターガール
erebētā gāru

Usually gigantic and luxurious, **depāto** (department stores) feature floors and floors of everything imaginable from kimonos to **nurimono** (lacquerware), as well as art galleries, restaurants and flower shops. Stylish sales staff and **erebētā gāru** (elevator ladies) are everywhere, ready to assist. Mitsukoshi is Japan's oldest depāto.

八
hachi
8

オ 
o

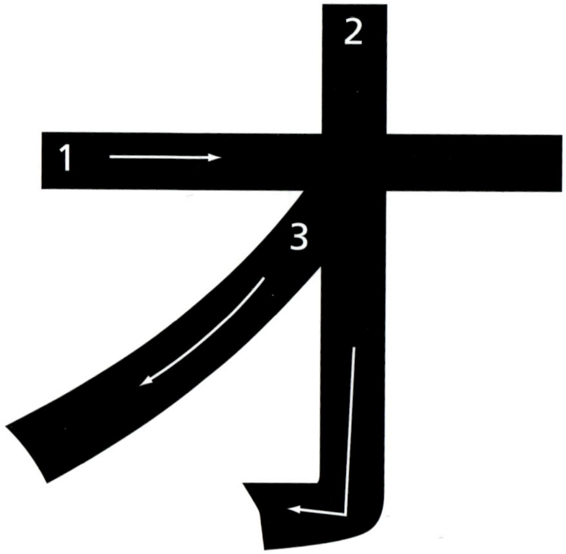

オートバイ
ōtobai

ヘルメット
herumetto

オートバイ
ōtobai

寿司

九
kyū
9

← カラオケボックス
karaoke bokkusu

カ

ka

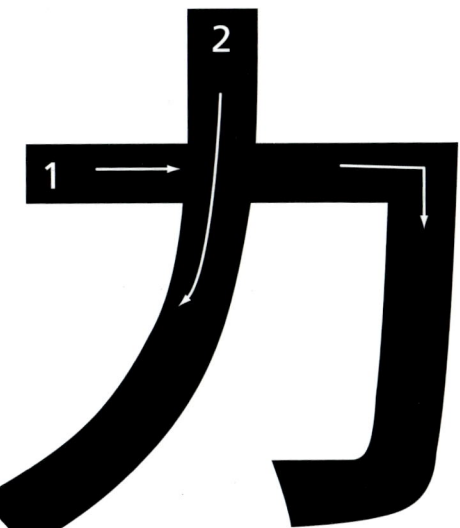

↑ カラオケ
karaoke

カラオケ
karaoke

Japanese love to sing **karaoke**. There are special requirements: 1) Everyone is expected to sing at least once; 2) Never sing without being asked; 3) Never sing more than once, unless asked. At the end of your performance, a **karaoke bokkusu** (karaoke machine) will rate your performance from **saikō** (best) to **heta** (terrible).

キ
ki

キヨスク
kiyosuku

えきべん
ekiben

カン コーヒー
kan kōhī

In train and subway stations there are **kiyosuku** (kiosks) where you can purchase manga, **shinbun** (newspapers), salty **sunakku** (snacks) and lots of **atsui** (hot) and **tsumetai** (cold) drinks, including **kan kōhī** (canned coffee) and **kenkō dorinku** (energy drinks). Some kiyosuku offer special **ekiben** (boxed lunch), noodles or sushi.

ク
ku

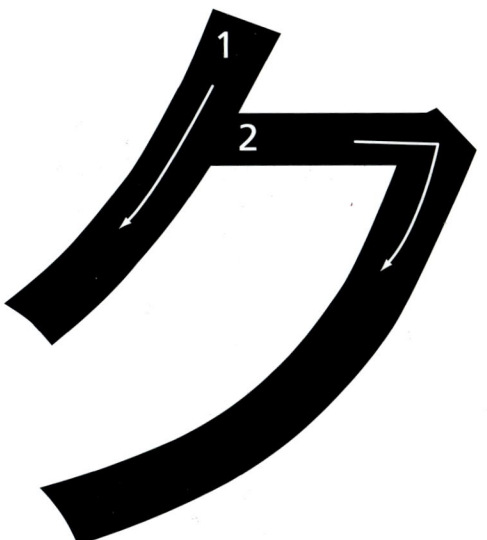

クリスマス
kurisumasu

↑
サンタクロース
santakurōsu

← クリスマス プレゼント
kurisumasu purezento

十二
jū ni
12

コ
ko

パスポートしゃしん
pasupōto shashin

コンビニ
konbini

おかし
okashi

Japanese **konbini** (convenience stores) are just that—convenient. On nearly every corner, konbini provide concert tickets, **pasupōto shashin** (passport photos) and **shiharai** (bill payment). Shelves are piled high with everything from **okashi** (snack food) to **zasshi** (magazines). Konbini are open 24 hours a day, 365 days a year.

十四
jū yon
14

サ
sa

サラリーマン
sarariman

七三わけ
shichisan wake

サラリーマン
sarariman

Japan has a lifetime employment system. Under it, **sarariman** (businessmen) are promised a regular salary and in return are loyal to a single company for life. Life of a sarariman is highly stressful. Many sarariman are obsessed with success, work long hours and, as a result, have little time for family and leisure activities.

シ
shi

シャワー
shawā

タオル
taroru

ふろおけ
furo oke

For decades, **sentō** (public bath) was the only way to bathe. In 1982, there were 13,050 sentō throughout Japan; now, only 5,759 remain. Today, most Japanese homes are equipped with bathrooms that include **toire** (toilet), **shawā** (shower) and **furo oke** (tub). Still, sentō plays an important role as a spot to relax and interact with neighbors.

ス
su

ス
1
2

スキー
sukī

スキー → sukī

Shaped like a gigantic **sukī** (ski) jump and sprinkled with crispy, crackly snow, Tokyo Sukī Dome, the world's largest indoor sukī and **snobō** (snowboarding) facility, was dreamed up in the 1990s as a year-round winter playground. At its peak, Tokyo Sukī Dome drew more than a million sukī and snobō enthusiasts per year.

*Editor's Note: The Tokyo Ski Dome is set to be demolished. The future site will be used for business developments.

タ
ta

タクシーのりば
takushī noriba

タクシー
takushī

← タクシー
takushī

Japanese **takushī** (taxi) are quite an experience. Takushī are incredibly clean, and many drivers wear white gloves. A number of takushī are spruced up to include extra perks like **terebi** (televisions), dvd players, sunakku and **oshibori** (moist towels) for your convenience. To signal a takushī, just raise your hand and one will stop.

二十
nijū

チ
chi

チ

チーム
chīmu

あかチーム
aka chīmu

しろチーム
shiro chīmu

In Japanese society, order, discipline and **chīmu wāku** (team work) are highly valued, as well as respect for age, experience and rank. Ancient Japanese proverbs describe chīmu wāku best: "The nail that sticks up gets hammered down" and "Better to be like bamboo, which bends in the wind, but never breaks."

←ツーリスト
tsūrisuto

ツ
tsu

ツーリスト
tsūrisuto

←ツアーガイド
tsuā gaido

For much of the Edo period, Japan kept out visitors. Today, millions of **tsūrisuto** (tourists) flock to Nihon to absorb its mysterious culture. Many visit Kyoto, Japan's imperial capital from 794 to 1868. Rich with culture, Kyoto features centuries old temples, lush Japanese gardens, and an abundance of Japanese arts and crafts.

テ
te

テレビ
terebi

リモート コントロール
remōto kontorōru

テレビ
terebi

大相撲

In 1953, the first program on Japanese **terebi** (television) was **kabuki** (traditional Japanese theater). Today, **jidaigeki** (samurai dramas), sumo, puro yakyū and **nyūsu** (news) are just a few of the many popular terebi shows. There are more than 100 million terebi throughout Japan. **Nani miteru?** (What are you watching?)

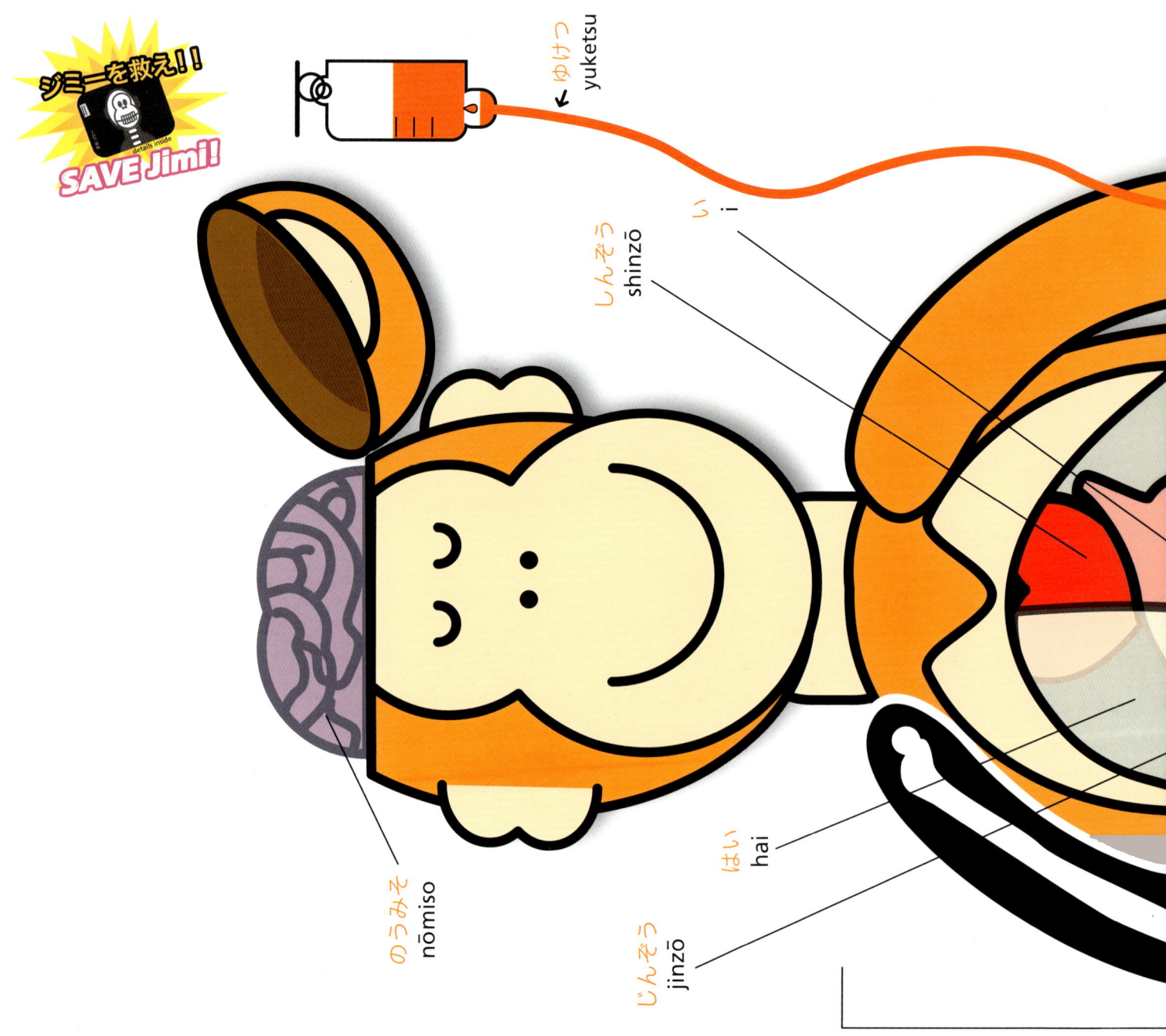

NOTE: This diagram uses both hiragana and katakana words. Hiragana words are shown in orange; katakana words are in blue.

かんぞう kanzō
だいちょう daichō
しょうちょう shōchō
きりきず kirikizu
ほうこう bōkō
ほね hone
こっせつ kottsetsu
レントゲン rentogen

organs: nōmiso—brain; shinzō—heart; i—stomach; kanzō—liver; daichō—large intestine; shōchō—small intestine; hone—bones; bōkō—bladder; jinzō—kidney; hai—lung
ailments: kirikizu—cut; kottsetsu—fracture
objects: rentogen—X-ray; yuketsu—blood transfusion

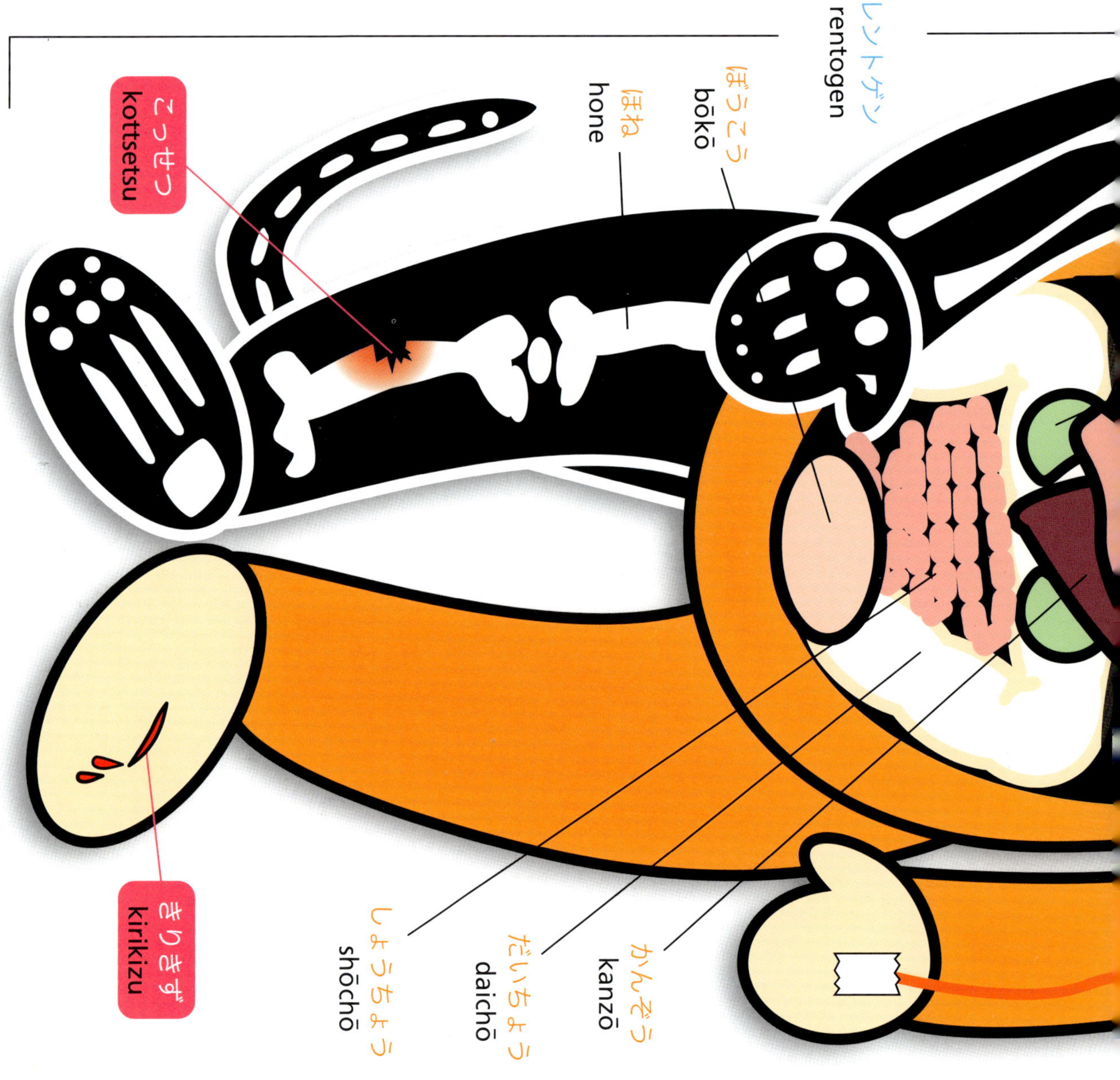

ヌ
nu

ヌードル
nūdoru

つきみうどん ↗
tsukimi udon

Nūdoru (noodles) are to Japanese what hamburgers are to Americans. In the 9th century, China introduced udon, a yummy nūdoru made from wheat flour, to Japan. Served hot or cold with special dipping sauce, udon also is topped with tempura, **tsukimi** (raw egg), **yamakake** (taro root), **yasai** (vegetables) and **niku** (meat).

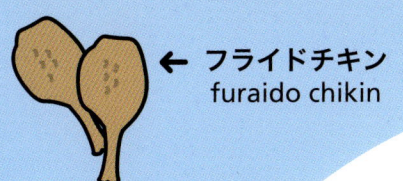 ← フライドチキン
furaido chikin

ハ
ha

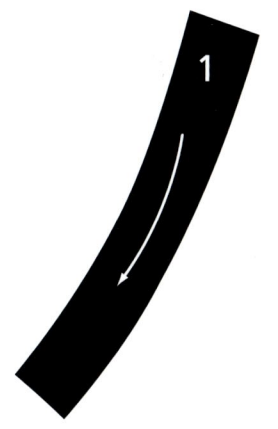
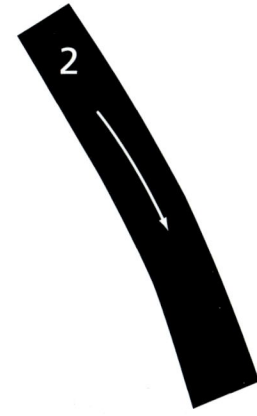

ハンバーガー
hanbāgā

フライドポテト
furaido poteto
↓

 ← ハンバーガー
hanbāgā

One of Nihon's legendary fast food restaurants is Mos Burger®, a chain of **hanbāgā** (hamburger) joints. Founded in 1972 by Satoshi Sakurada, Mos Burger® offers 21 tasty hanbāgā varieties, from teriyaki to tofu, topped with secret sauce and toasty rice buns. Charge yourself with Japanese joy. Eat Mos Burger®!

Mos Burger® MOS Food Services, Inc.

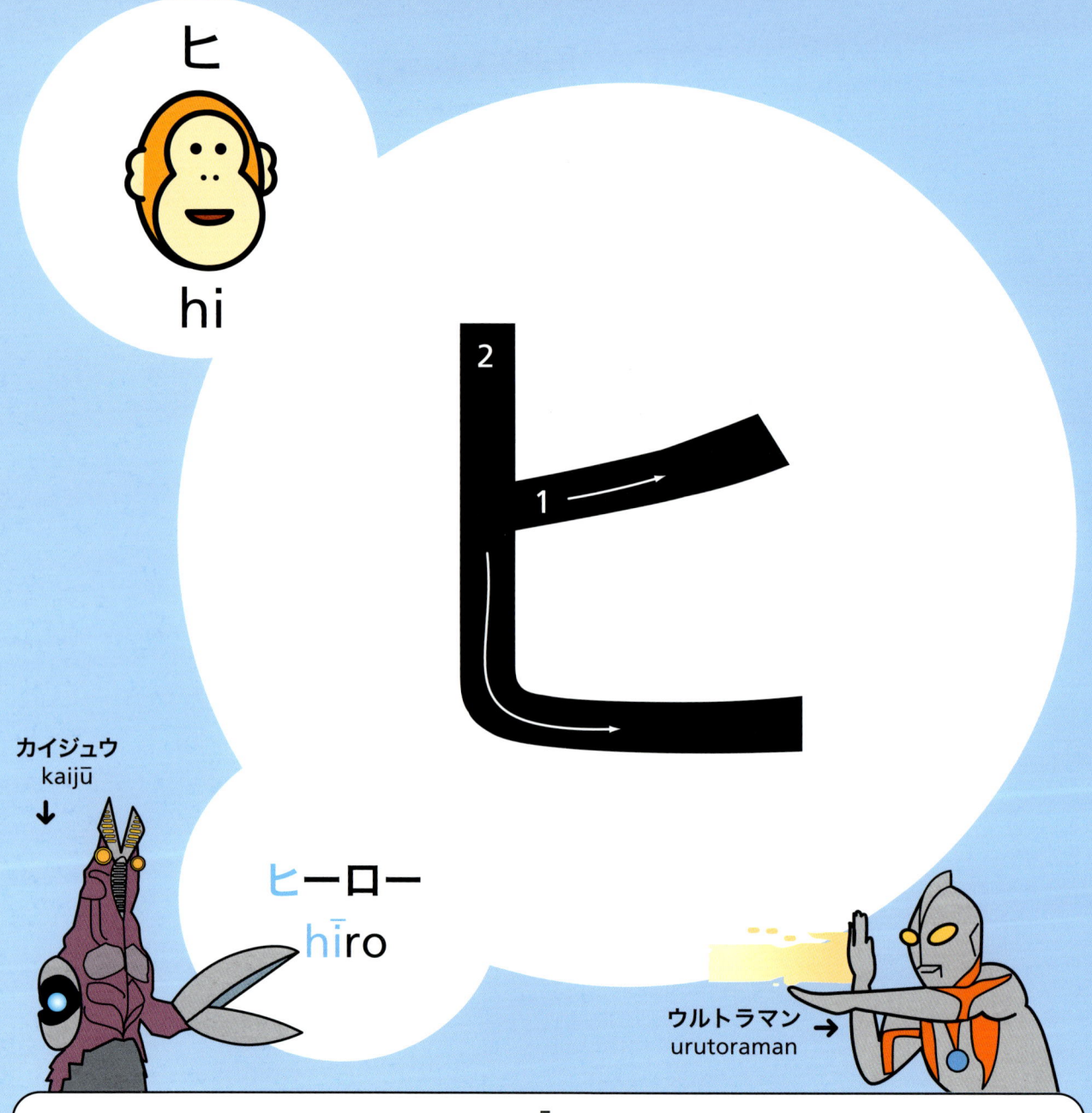

ヒ
hi

カイジュウ
kaijū

ヒーロー
hīro

ウルトラマン
urutoraman

Why is Nihon so safe? Main reason: **sūpā hīro** (super heroes). Superhuman powers allow hīro to defeat any menace from scary **kaijū** (monsters) to sinister brains floating in jars of goo. Japan's greatest sūpā hīro is Ultraman®, a kaijū-fighting sensation whose Spacium ray destroys evil-doers with a single blast. "Shuwatch!"

ULTRAMAN®Tsuburaya Productions Co., Ltd.

ゴルフボール
gorufu bōru

フ
fu

ゴルフ
gorufu

ゴルフクラブ
gorufu kurabu

In the 20th century, **gorufu** (golf) was introduced to Japan. Today, gorufu is hugely popular with more 12 million golfers. **Gorufu jyō** (golf courses) are always busy and it is difficult to reserve a tee time. Membership at a prestigious gorufu jyō costs more than several years' salary and, in some cases, billions of yen.

へ

he

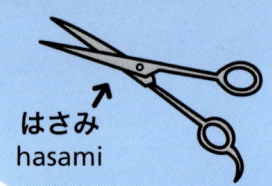
はさみ
hasami

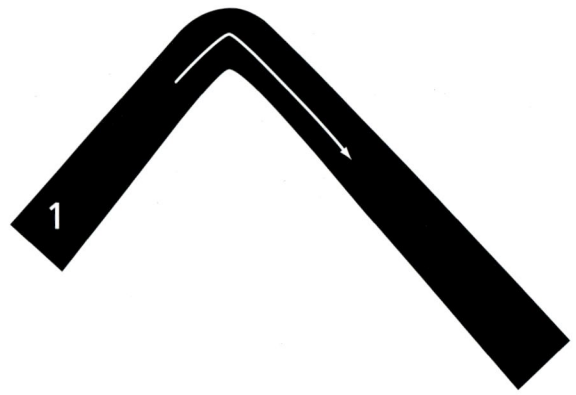

ヘアーカット
heākatto

ボブ
bobu

レイヤー
reiyā

ストレート
sutorēto

ツンツン
tsuntsun

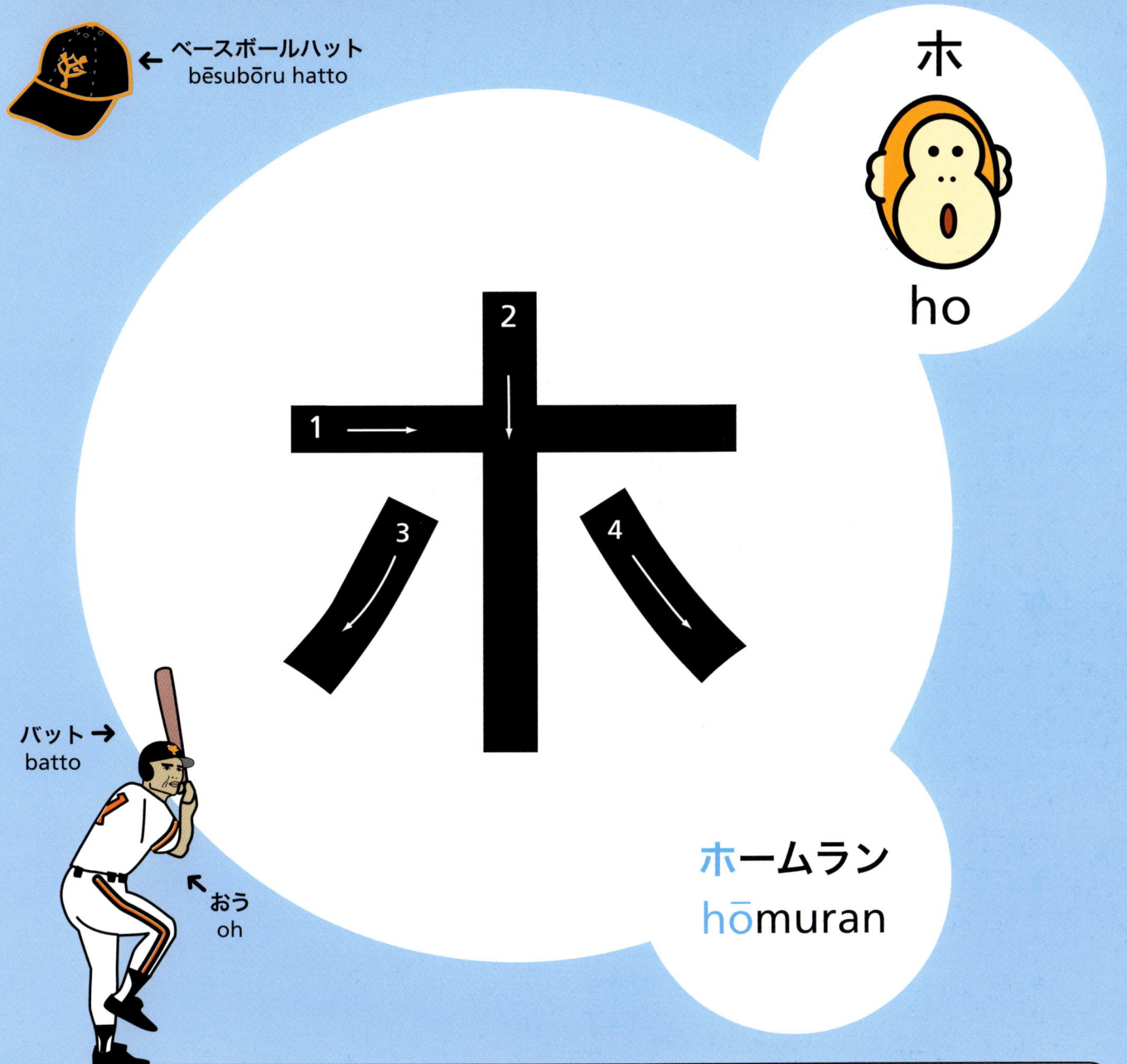

ベースボールハット
bēsubōru hatto

ホ
ho

バット
batto

おう
oh

ホームラン
hōmuran

A nine-time MVP first baseman for the Tokyo Giants, Sadaharu Oh is a Japanese **puro yakyū** (pro baseball) legend. During his career, the "Flamingo" belted 868 **hōmuran** (home runs), smacked 2,786 **hitto** (hits) and drove in 2,170 **ten** (runs). View the bats he used to hit hōmuran #756 and #800 on display at the Baseball Hall of Fame, Tokyo.

マ

ma

マ

マスク
masuku

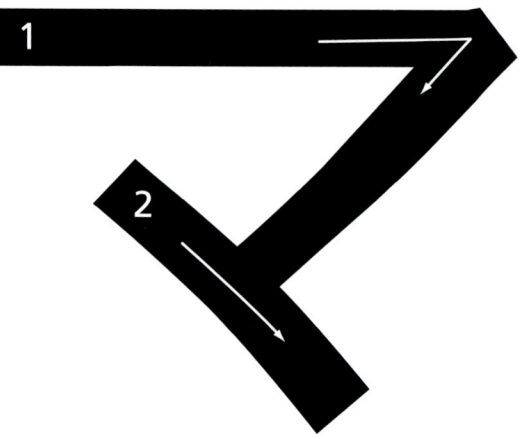

かんごふさん
kangofu san
マスク
masuku
マスク
masuku

マスク
masuku

ミ

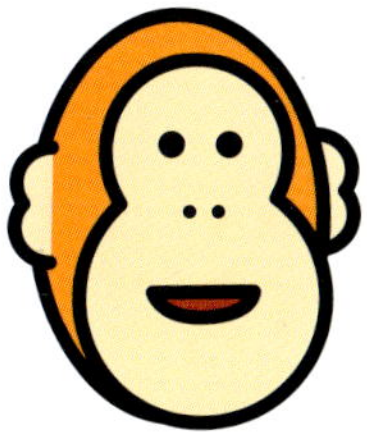

mi

1
2
3

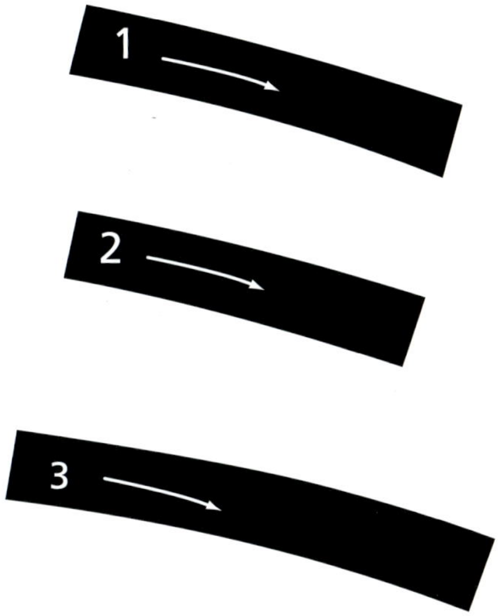

ミニ

mini

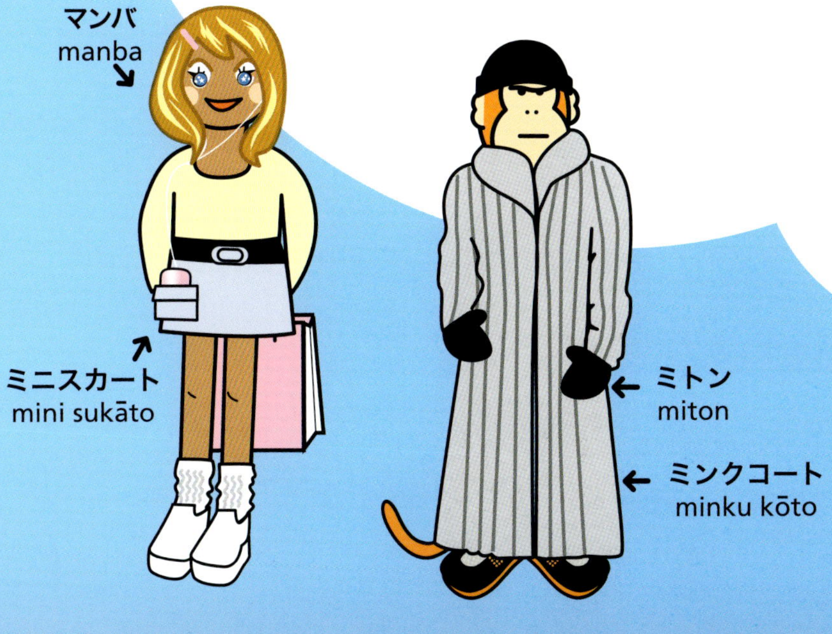

マンバ
manba
ミニスカート
mini sukāto
ミトン
miton
ミンクコート
minku kōto

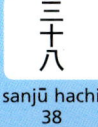

ム
mu

ゲーム
gēmu

ゲーム → gēmu

ご ゲーム → go gēmu

Thirteen hundred years ago, China introduced **Go**, a complex strategy **gēmu** (game), to Japan. Go is an indoor board game in which two people alternately place black and white stones on a board as they try to capture an opponent's stones or surround him completely. Go is wildly popular, with more than ten million players throughout Japan.

モ

mo

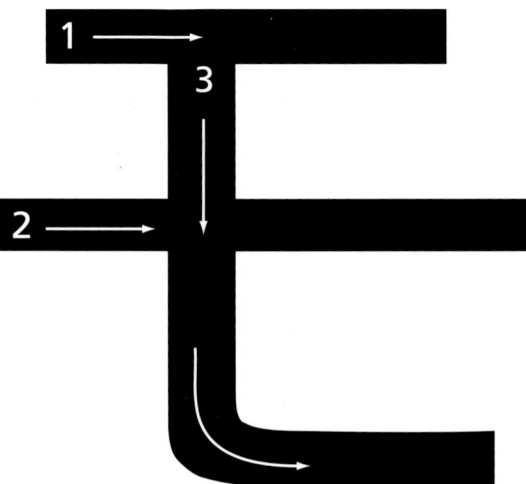

モーニング
mōningu

おはよう
ohayō
モーニング
mōningu

こんにちは
konnichiwa
アフターヌーン
afutā nūn

こんばんは
konbanwa
ナイト
naito

ヤ
ya

ヤ

ヤンキース
yankīsu

のも nomo
イチロー ichiro
まつい matsui

Japanese **yakyū** is regarded as a moral discipline rather than a game. Its purpose is to develop purity and self-discipline through endless training, self-denial and **wa** (team spirit). Today, many Japanese yakyū stars play in America: Hideo Nomo, L.A. Dodgers; Ichiro Suzuki, Seattle Mariners; and Hideki Matsui, New York Yankīsu (Yankees).

四十二
yonjū ni
42

ユ

yu

ユニフォーム
yunifōmu

つめえり
tsumeeri

セーラーふく
sērā fuku

In the late 19th century, Japan introduced school **yunifōmu** (uniforms) as part of its modernization efforts. Today, the school uniform is part of conventional Japanese life. A school uniform consists of a **tsumeeri** (military style) for boys and a **sērā fuku** (sailor dress) for girls. Different schools in Japan are known for their style of uniform.

ラ
ra

ラ

ランドセル
randoseru

ランドセル
randoseru

The first day of elementary school in Japan is a ceremonial occasion. Gifts are customary; **randoseru** (leather backpack) is given by a student's relatives to commemorate the landmark occasion. Everything from **enpitsu** (pencils) to nōto are stored in randoseru. **Kuro** (black) randoseru is for otokonoko, **aka** (red) for onnanoko.

リサイクル
risaikuru

↑ リサイクル risaikuru ↑ ペットボトル petto botoru ↑ プラスチック purasuchikku

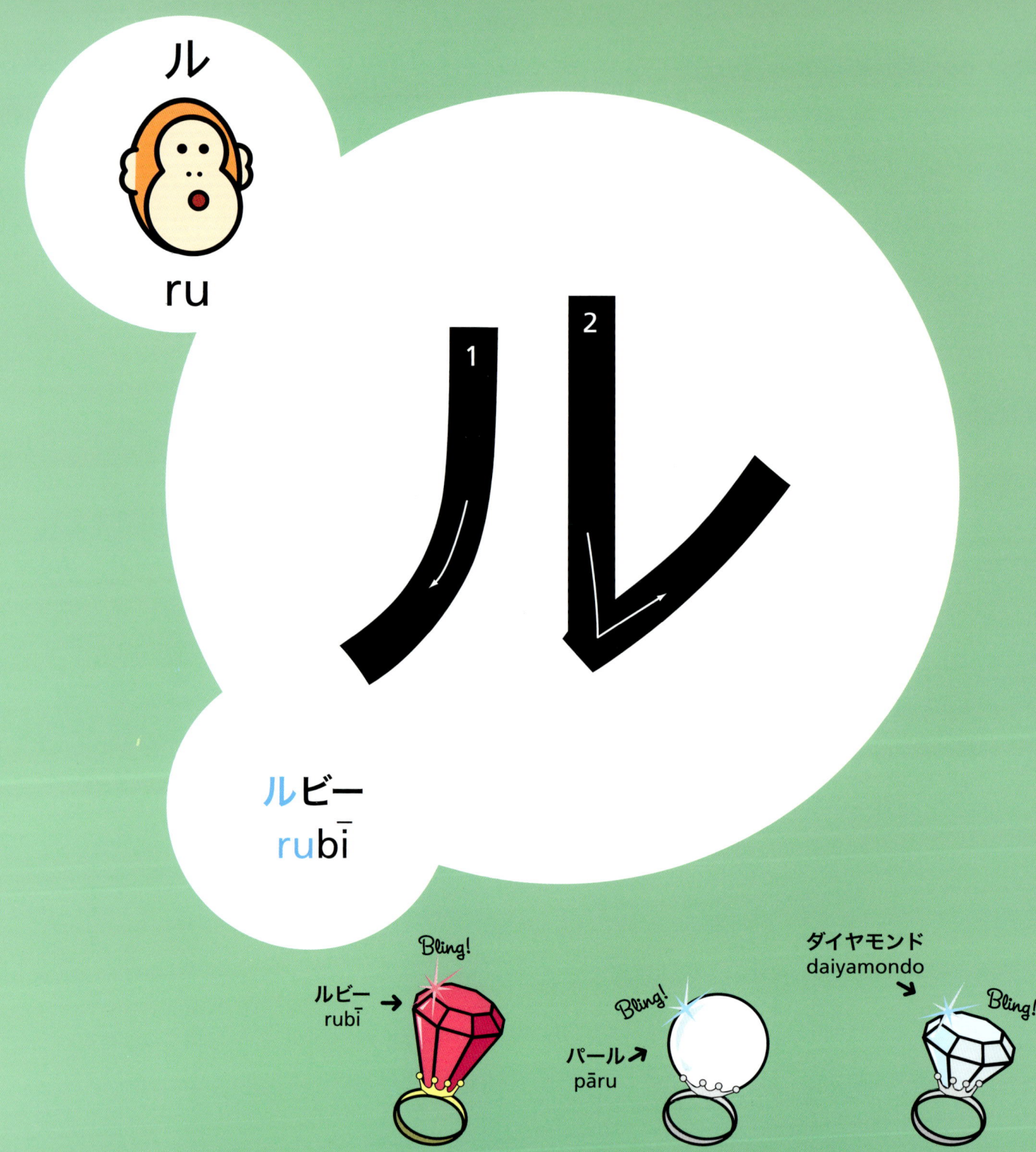

レ
re

レコード
rekōdo

ディージェー
DJ

レコード
rekōdo

キュッ キュッ
kyutt kyutt

Follow the trendsetters to Udagawa-cho, a hyper-crowded Tokyo alleyway crammed from street to sky with **rekōdo shoppu** (record shops). Step inside rekōdo shoppu and rummage through stacks of the freshest wax from Hip-hop and Old School to Trance and House while international DJs mix funky beats with growling bass lines.

四十八
yonjū hachi
48

ロ
ro

ロボット
robotto

ろぼっと さん
robotto-san

アイボ
aibo

Ever met a robotto? Say ohayō to AIBO®, Sony's fascinating robotic **petto** (pet). Designed to resemble a lion cub, AIBO® can dance and express its emotions through green happy lights, a wagging tail and lifelike body language. AIBO® can even recharge itself. Teach AIBO® tricks and it will become a loyal and realistic companion.

AIBO® Sony Corporation

四十九
yonjū kyū
49

ワ
wa

タワー
tawā

ゴジラ
gojira

とうきょうタワー
tokyo tawā

In **eiga** (movies), Godzilla® snapped Tokyo **Tawā** (tower) in two. In reality, the monstrous structure is open for tours offering a view of Tokyo from 250m up. Tokyo Tawā also features an aquarium, a wax museum and an art gallery. Built in 1958, Tokyo Tawā is the world's tallest self-supporting structure—even taller than the Eiffel Tawā.

Godzilla®©Toho Co., Ltd.

五十
gojū
50

ヲ
WO

ヲ
(w)o

五十一
gojū ichi
51

あんパンマン ← anpanman

ン n

パン pan

あんパン anpan →

パン pan →

Anpan, a scrumptious creation of **pan** (bread) filled with **an** (red bean paste), is Japan's most popular pastry. Anpanman®, a superhero made of anpan, is one of Japan's most popular anime. In each episode, Anpanman® fights villains, protects the weak and feeds the hungry by allowing them to eat his tasty face. "AN-PUNCH!" "AN-KICK!"

Anpanman®© Takashi Yanase

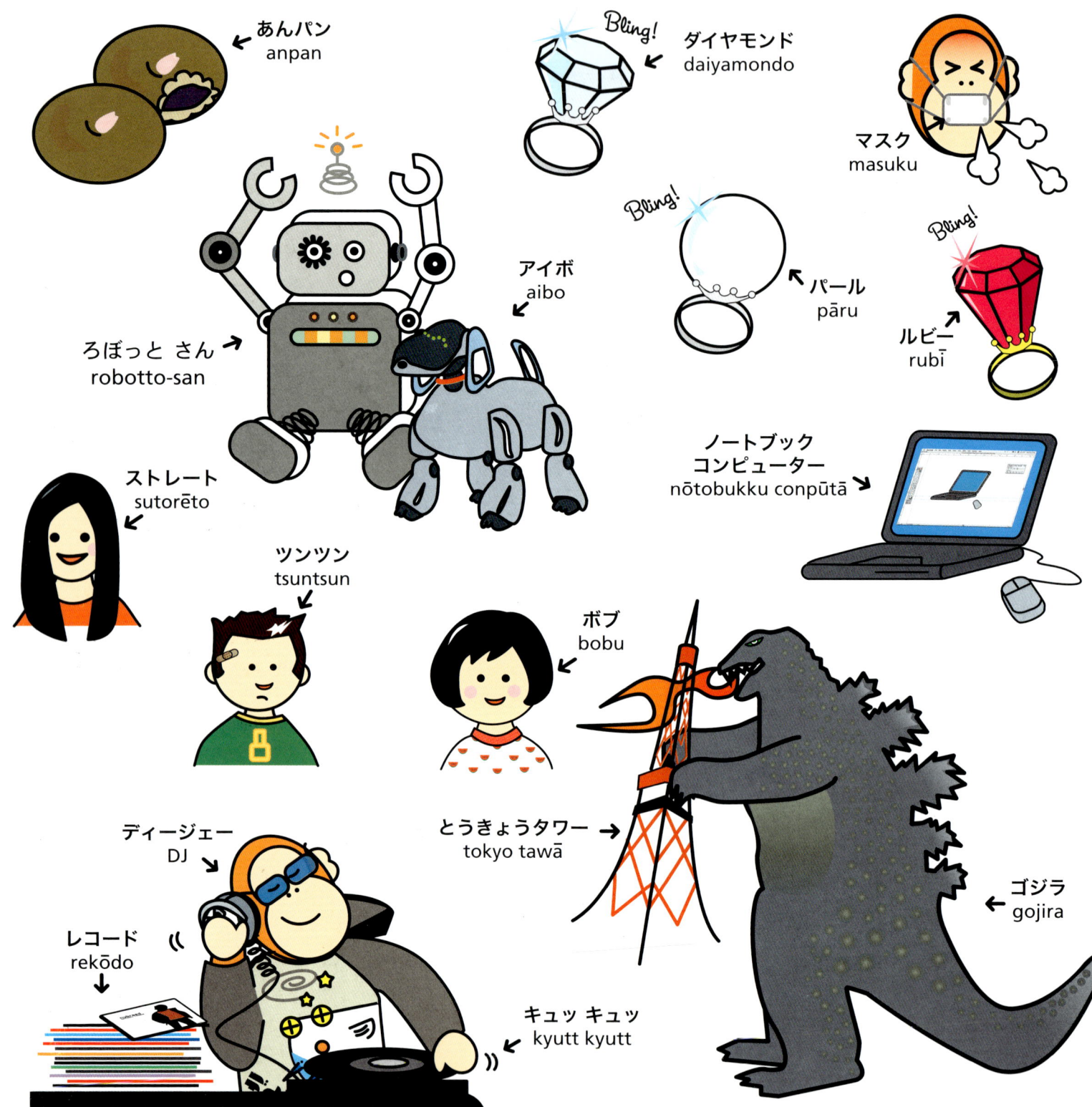

Numbers

十	jū 10	
二十	ni jū 20	 
三十	san jū 30	  
四十	yon jū 40	
五十	go jū 50	
六十	roku jū 60	
七十	nana jū 70	  
八十	hachi jū 80	   
九十	kyū jū 90	 
百	hyaku 100	

Numbers shown in yen, the official currency of Japan.

Word List

A	afutā nūn	afternoon
	aka	red
	aka chīmu	red team
	an	red bean paste
	anime	Japanese animation
	anime kyarakutā	anime character
	anpan	bread filled with red bean paste
	anpanman	bean powered superhero
	atsui	hot; hot drink
B	batto	baseball bat
	bēsubōru hatto	baseball hat
	bōkō	bladder
	buinekku sētā	v-neck sweater
	bunkintakashimada	special wedding hairdo
C	cherī tomato	cherry tomato
	chīmu	team
	chīmu wāku	team work
	chō nekutai	bow tie
D	daichō	large intestine
	depāto	department store
	daiyamondo	diamond
	dorinku	drink(s)
E	eiga	movies
	ekiben	special boxed lunch sold at train stations
	erebētā gāru	elevator girl
F	fōku	fork
	fugu	blowfish; puffer fish
	furaido chikin	fried chicken
	furaido poteto	fried potatoes
	furo oke	bath tub
G	gēmu	game
	go	traditional board game
	gorufu	golf
	gorufu bōru	golf ball
	gorufu kurabu	golf club
H	hai	lung
	hanbāgā	hamburger
	hasami	scissors
	herumetto	helmet
	heta	terrible
	hinomaru	Japanese national flag
	hīrō	hero
	hone	bone

I	**i**	stomach
	ichigo	strawberry
	iruka	dolphin, porpoise
	intānetto	Internet
J	**jidaigeki**	samurai dramas
	jinzō	kidney
K	**kabuki**	traditional Japanese theater
	kaijū	monster(s)
	kan kōhī	canned coffee
	kana	Japanese syllabary
	kangofu san	nurse
	kanzō	liver
	karaoke	karaoke
	karaoke bokkusu	karaoke machine
	katakana	sounds Japanese has borrowed from other languages
	kēki	cake
	kenkō dorinku	health drink(s)
	kimono	traditional Japanese dress
	kiyosuku	kiosk
	kirikizu	scrape, cut
	kōhī	coffee
	konbanwa	Good evening!
	konbini	convenience store
	konnichiwa	Good afternoon!
	kottsetsu	bone fracture
	kurisumasu	Christmas
	kurisumasu puresento	Christmas presents
	kurūnekku sētā	crew-neck sweater
	kyutt kyutt	onomatopoeia
M	**manba**	rare fashion subculture among teens
	masuku meron	musk melon
	media mēru	media mail
	mini sukāto	mini skirt
	minku	mink
	miton	mitten
	mōningu	morning
	montsuki	black kimono with family crest
N	**naifu**	knife
	naito	night
	nekkuresu	necklace
	nekutai	necktie
	niku	meat
	ninjin	carrot
	ninniku	garlic
	nira	Korean chives
	nōto	notebook
	nōto bukku konpūtā	notebook computer
	nōmiso	brain
	nūdoru	noodle(s)

	nurimono	lacquerware
	nyūsu	news
O	**ohayō**	Good morning!
	okashi	snack food
	oshibori	moist towelettes
	ōtobai	motorbike
P	**pan**	bread
	pāru	pearl
	pasupōto	passport
	pasupōto shashin	passport photo
	petto botoru	PET bottle
	purasuchikku	recyclable plastic
	purezento	presents
	purinsu meron	prince melon; tiny melon
	puro yakyū	pro baseball
R	**randoseru**	leather backpack
	rekōdo	record
	rekōdo shoppu	record shop
	remōto kontorōru	remote control
	rentogen	X-ray
	risaikuru	recycle; recyclable
	roketto	rocket
	rubī	ruby
S	**saikō**	best
	sararīman	salaryman; white-collar worker
	sentō	public bath
	sērā fuku	sailor-style school uniform
	sētā	sweater
	shashin	photograph
	shawā	shower
	shichisan wake	seven-three salaryman hairstyle
	shiharai	bill payment
	shinbun	newspaper
	shinzō	heart
	shiro	white
	shiro chīmu	white team
	shiromuku	wedding dress
	shōchō	small intestine
	shūgibukuro	special decorative envelope
	snobō	snowboard, snowboarding
	sofā	sofa
	sukī	ski
	sunakku	snack(s)
	supūn	spoon
	sushi	rice seasoned with vinegar, topped with fish or vegetables
T	**takushī**	taxi
	takushī noriba	taxi stand
	tātorunekku sētā	turtleneck sweater
	ten/tokuten	run (baseball term)

	tenpura	tempura
	terebi	television
	toire	toilet
	tomato	tomato
	toumorokoshi	corn
	tsuā	tour
	tsuā gaido	tour guide
	tsukimi udon	udon noodle soup with raw egg
	tsumeeri	military-style school uniform
	tsumetai	cold; cool drink
	tsunokakushi	wedding headdress
	tsūrisuto	tourist
U	**uchū**	universe
	udon	wheat noodles
	uedingu	wedding
W	**wa**	team spirit
	wāku	work
Y	**yakyū**	baseball
	yamakake	graded taro root over noodles
	yankīsu	Yankees
	yasai	vegetables
	yen	Japanese currency
	yotto	yacht
	yūbari meron	famous Hokkaido melon
	yuketsu	blood transfusion
Z	**zasshi**	magazines

Katakana Chart

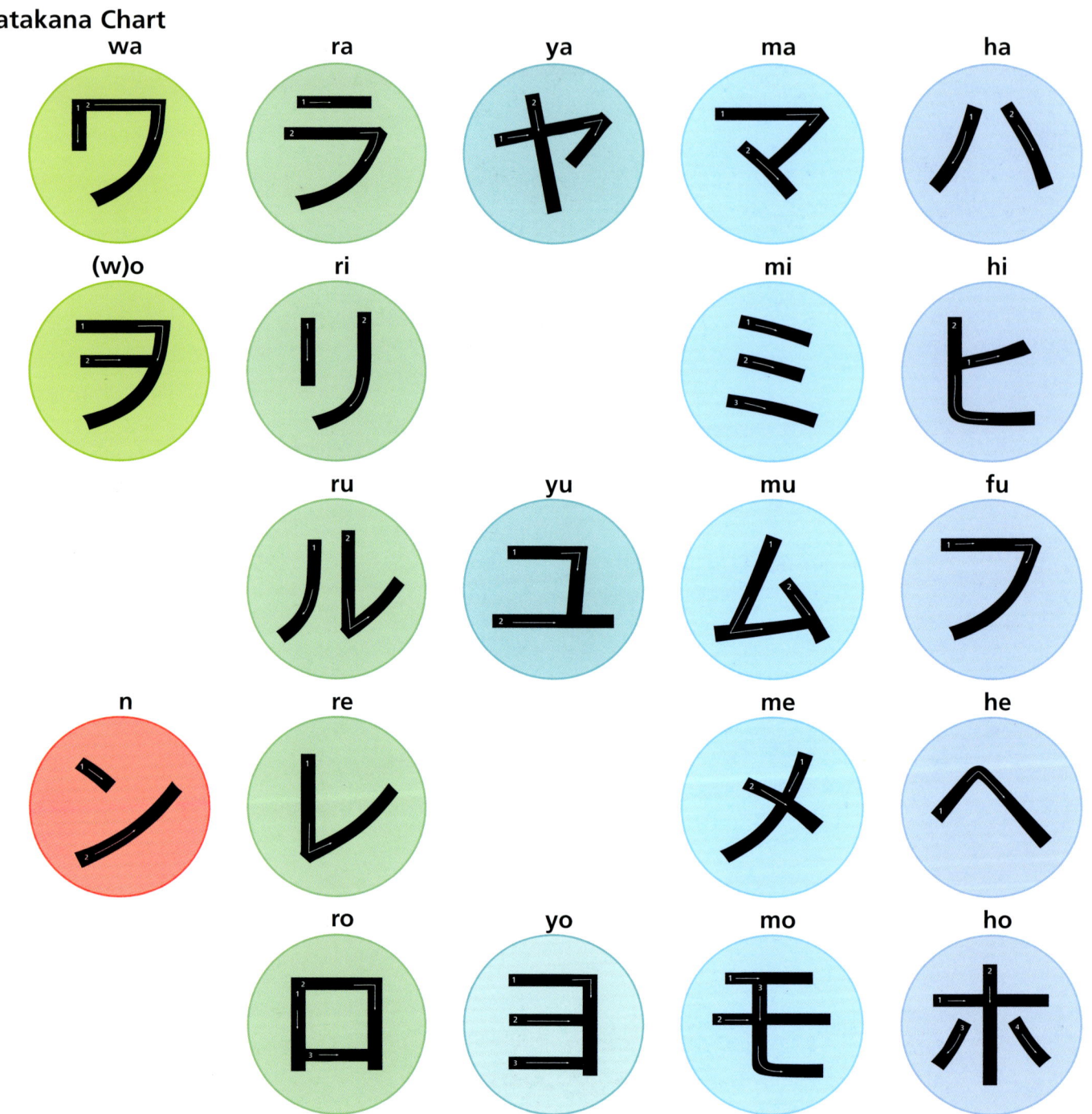

This chart is presented Japanese-style. Start on the right-hand page. Read from top to bottom, then right to left.
NOTE: The syllables **yi**, **ye**, **wi**, **wu** and **we** do not exist in modern Japanese.

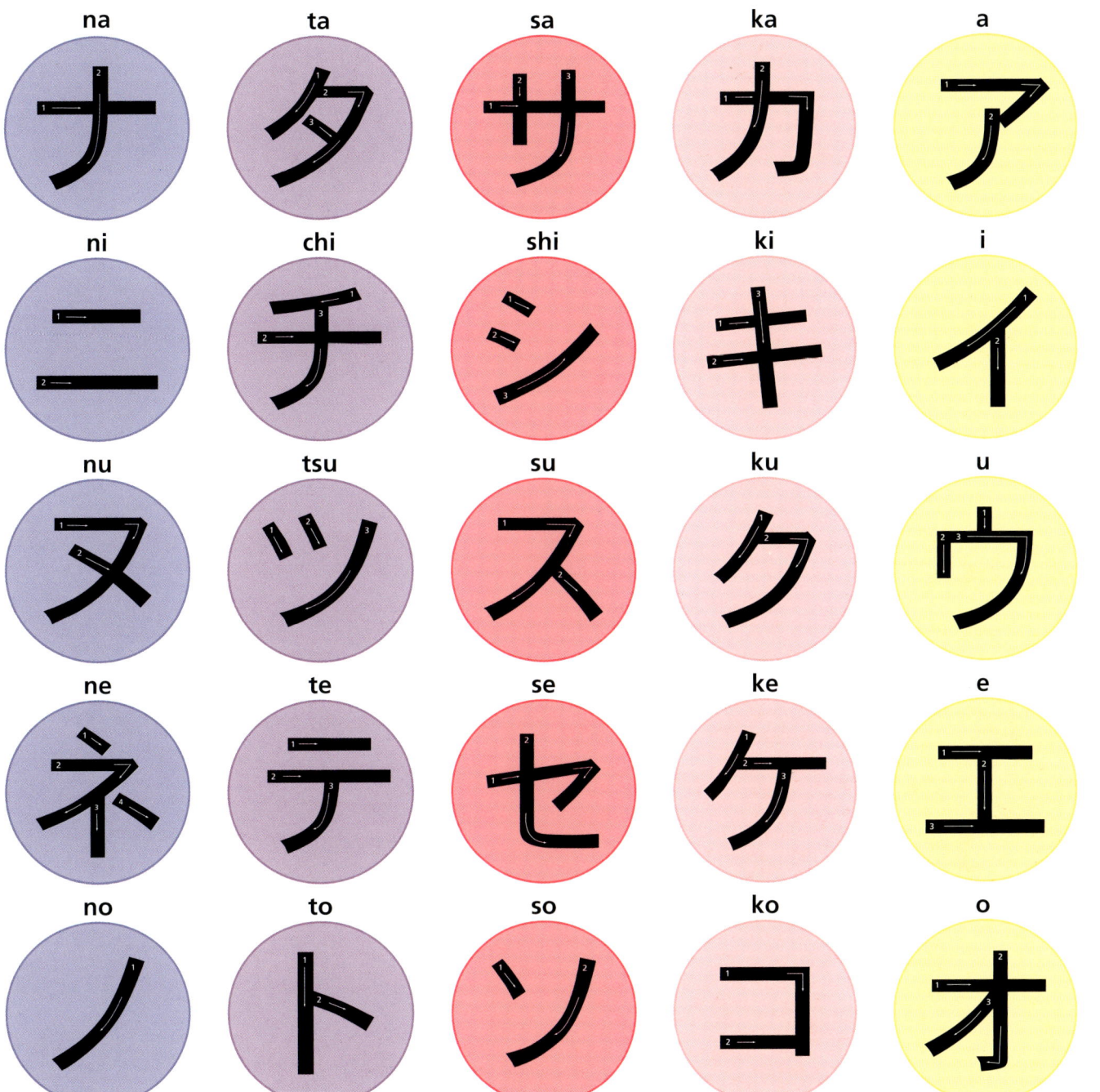

Authors' acknowledgements

I would like to send big, big thanks to Yumie for her unique blend of insight, imagination and intelligent technique in creating and articulating the Jimi brand. Thanks also to my folks and family, Ted No. 33, Chucklehead Fred, Mr. PBJ, a woman named Moto, Yama-san, Elliott Staples, Kathleeeeen 'Everything Goes With' O'Brien, Satoshi and Midori, Honda-san, Fried Chicken and everyone who supported (and continues to support) the Jimi empire.
— Peter X. Takahashi

• • •

Many, many thanks to Andrew and Isaac for their incurable curiosity and tireless motivation on this project. Thanks also to my parents, aunt Mako, Daisuke & Miki, Sylvia, Katherine Buttler, Maki Manning, Daniel Wong and Señor Rohde-san. Special thanks to Peter X. for his wit, wisdom, and drive that keep the Jimi dream alive.
— Yumie Toka

• • •

Many thanks to Yumie and Peter X. for inviting me into the world of Jimi and friends—I look forward to new adventures with this team. I want to thank my husband, family and friends who have spread the word about Jimi so that others can enjoy the lively, playful, and creative wit of the author and illustrator and find their lives—and coffee tables— enriched.
— Mikki Moto

アリガトウ
arigatō!

Peter X. Takahashi is an award-winning author, underrated DJ and soon-to-be-sought-after nightclub act. In his free time, PXT enjoys eating yakiniku, sculpting bonzai, playing gorufu and perfecting his Nimzo-Indian Defense. This is his third book. He lives and works in Tokyo.

peterx@pbjomnimedia.com

Yumie Toka is an award-winning illustrator and interaction designer whose trend-setting style is adored by kids, adults and monkeys around the world. In her spare time, Yumie enjoys yoga, meditation and teaching her two boys karate, kung fu and a whole bunch of magic tricks. Born and raised in Tokyo, she lives and works in Atlanta. This is her third book.

yumiepower@pbjomnimedia.com

Mikki Moto is an accomplished editor with dozens of books to her credit. When she is not working, Mikki and her secret agent husband enjoy globetrottting in pursuit of the freshest wasabi peas and the world's spiciest super crunchy roll. Born and raised on water skis near Lake Biwa, Japan, she lives and works in Atlanta.

moto@pbjomnimedia.com

Visit **www.pbjomnimedia.com** for even more motivating methods to learn Japanese, Supaa Rare™ freebies and breaking news about other interactive PB&J products. Prepare your nōmiso. . .